Go God Go!

"In this wonderful book, Gene captures the joyful essence of the creation story in a way that will captivate the curious minds of children. *Go God Go!* celebrates the all-powerful God of creation, the joy of the Creator, and the beauty of creation with rhyme and lyric that will deeply engage the heart of every child who turns these pages. This book offers a fun way to teach the wonders of our Creator God to our children and grandchildren."

—STEVE BIONDO
President, Tim Tebow Foundation

Go God Go!

Words by: Gene Krcelic
Pictures by: Alyson Record

Ambassador International
Greenville, South Carolina & Belfast, Northern Ireland

www.ambassador-international.com

Go God Go!

©2019 Gene Krcelic
All rights reserved

Illustrated by Alyson Record

ISBN: 978-1-64960-799-7, hardcover
ISBN: 978-1-64960-689-1, paperback
eISBN: 978-1-62020-969-1

Page Layout: Hannah Nichols
Ebook Conversion: Anna Riebe Raats

AMBASSADOR INTERNATIONAL
Emerald House
411 University Ridge Suite B14,
Greenville, SC 29601, USA
www.ambassador-international.com

AMBASSADOR BOOKS
The Mount
2 Woodstock Link
Belfast, BT6 8DD, Northern Ireland, UK
www.ambassadormedia.co.uk

The colophon is a trademark of Ambassador, a Christian publishing company

Dedication

For Caroline, Alexis, and all children who love to explore their imagination in books.

Preface

I love a lyrically written and beautifully illustrated children's book. Through those books, the words and pictures come to life and settle within my imagination. I wanted to offer a fun and lyrical journey through the story of creation using the whimsical artwork of Alyson Record. My prayer is that your family will be inspired by our interpretation of God's work. My wife, Mary, and I read to our girls every night when they were growing up. Those books and the love between Jeff and Lindsay Oehman supplied the seed for *Go God Go!* Enjoy the journey. Buen Camino.

In the beginning,
the earth was cold and dark.
The dark was so dark you couldn't see a dog bark.
No barking, no whispers, no giggles, no laughs,
No trees, no people, not even giraffes.

Go God Go!

And then there was light,
The warm light was so bright,
so bright was the light,
It felt just right, what a welcome sight.
God had fun making day one,
making day one was so much fun.

Go God Go!

On day number two there was much to do!
Water below and water above,
The sky was clear but where was the dove?
Night time and morning, with day in between,
Water here, water there, but no land to be seen.

Go God Go!

On day number three
there was a lot to see.

God made the land,
and the land was so grand.
He made plants and trees,
that swayed in the breeze.
Tasty fruit and pretty green leaves,
And beautiful flowers
that grew up to your knees

Go God Go!

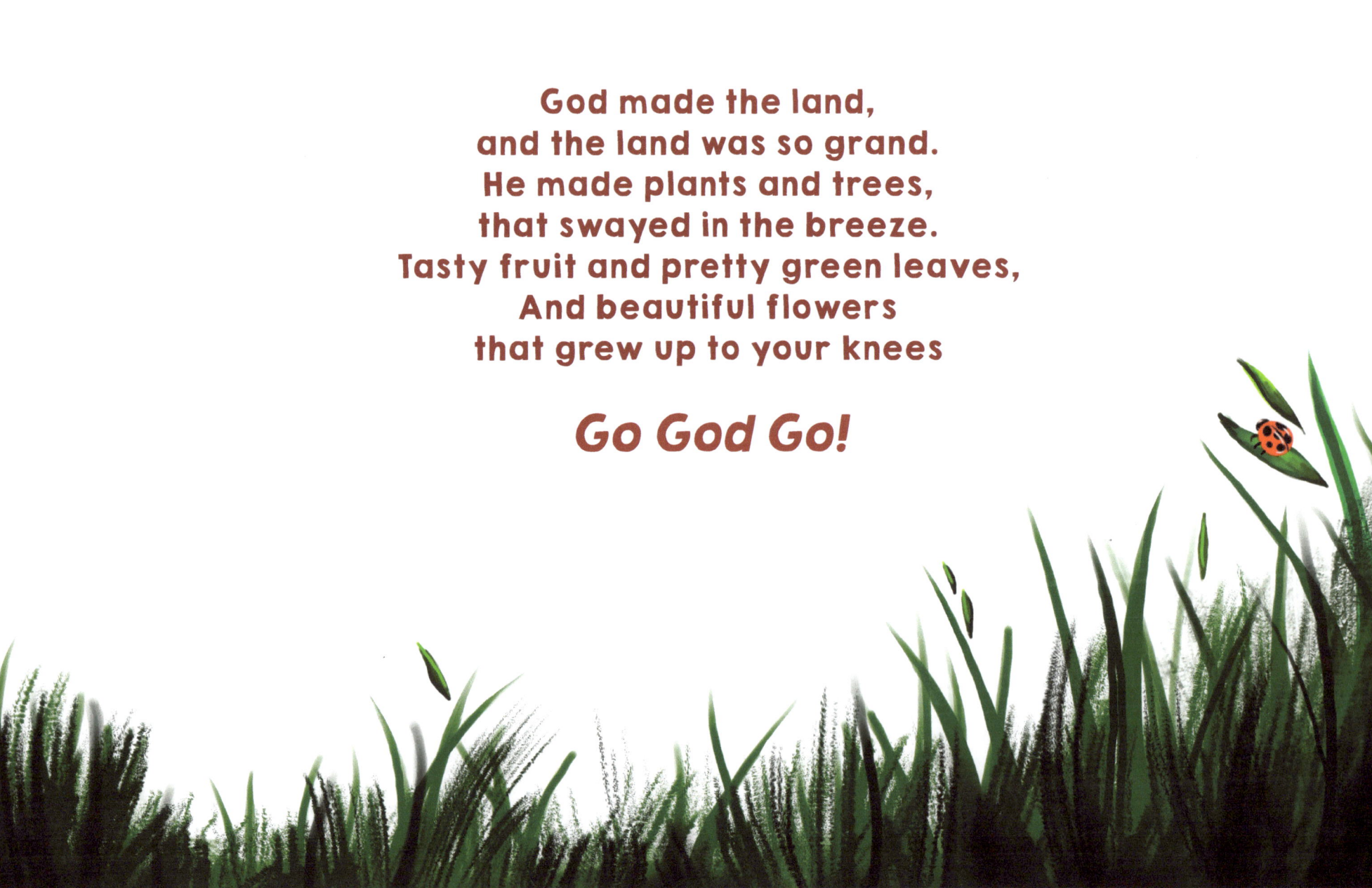

It was time
for the sun,
the moon,
and the stars,

Twinkling at night,
by the moon and by Mars.
Sunrise and sunset so colorful and pretty,
But still no white dove, what a pity.
It was good on day four,
but there had to be more,
there just had to be more,
more than day four.

Go God Go!

Day five came alive,
    Alive came day five.

Bird after bird flying high above the trees,
And millions of fish swimming under the seas.
So many fish and birds,
they were good beyond words,
God's creation was best,
but He still did not rest.

Go God Go!

Lions and horses and elephants everywhere!
A monkey, a kitten, a cow, and a bear.

On day number six,
God created the animal,
every creature, every reptile,
every insect, every mammal.
But He was not done,
oh He was not done,
He was not done with His good God fun!

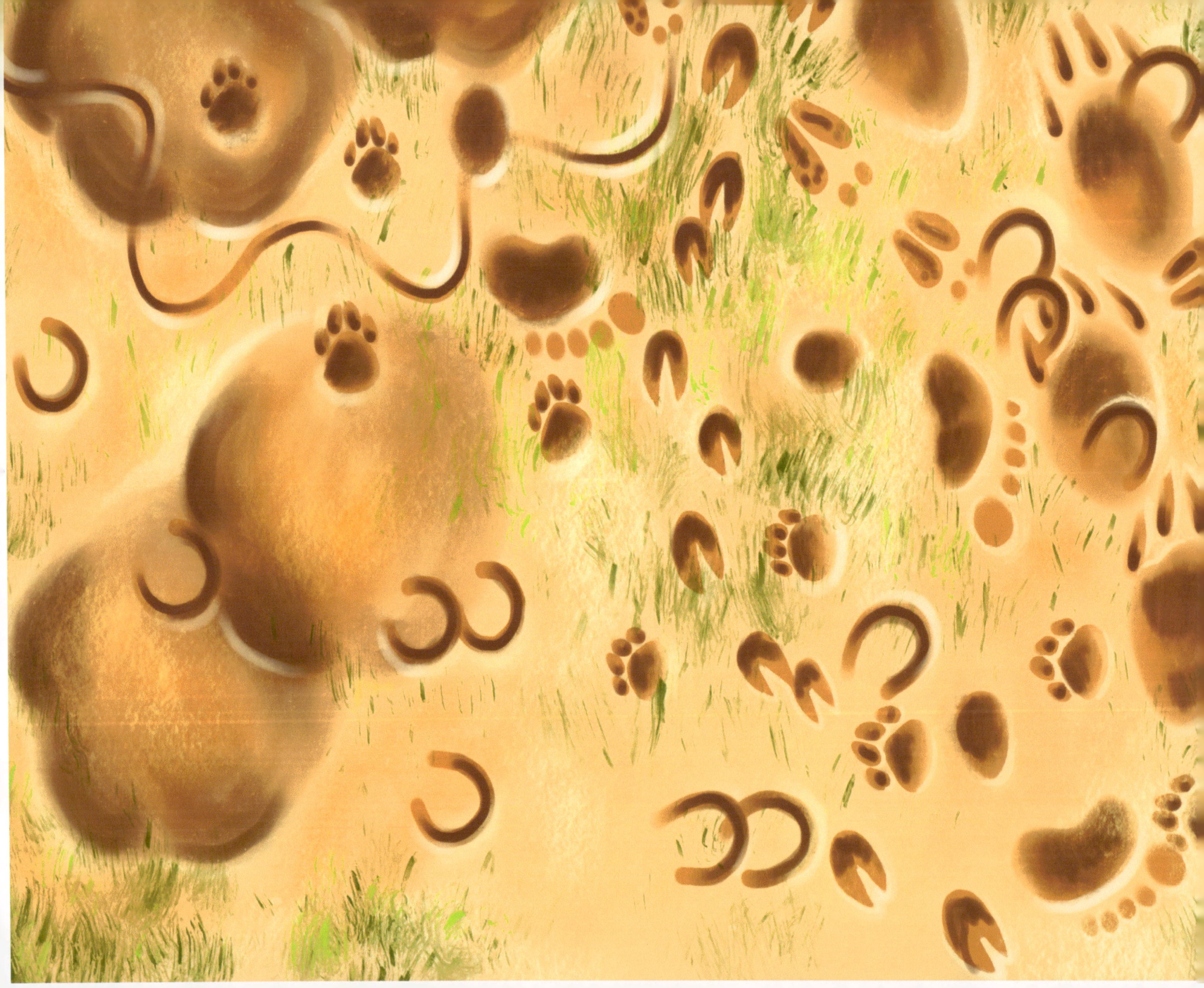

There still was time on
day number six,
just enough time to
finish the mix.

In His own image, God breathed into life,
Adam and Eve, the first man, the first wife.
And when the moon rose above the field and the wood,
God knew His creation was good, good, good!

Go God Go!

After all was complete,
on earth and in heaven,
God's creation was good,
so He rested on seven.

His love was everywhere,
below and above.
His love flew high,
on the wings of the dove.
A lot of work in a week don't ya think?
But for God, it was only a blink and a wink.

Go God Go!

Gene is a husband and father living in Greenville, South Carolina. He is President of the Premier Foundation, a non-profit charity committed to serving the world's impoverished. Gene is the author of the book, *Loves Like a Hurricane* (Ambassador International, 2010), and is working on a number of other writing projects inspired by the Bible, relationships, and his travels serving those in need.

Alyson is an emerging artist based in Nashville, TN. She loves bringing stories to life with her art and seeing the joy of others as they experience the story through her images. This is the second book she has illustrated. Alyson would like to thank God and her family for constant guidance and support in pursuing her craft.

To learn more about
Gene Krcelic

and
Go God Go!

please visit:
www.gogodgomedia.com
www.facebook.com/genekrcelic
@Krcelic

Instagram:
@gogodgomedia
@gkrcelic
@ajoy.art

For more information about
AMBASSADOR INTERNATIONAL
please visit:

www.ambassador-international.com

@AmbassadorIntl

www.facebook.com/AmbassadorIntl

www.ingramcontent.com/pod-product-compliance
Lightning Source LLC
LaVergne TN
LVHW071110070426
835507LV00004B/138